I0335564

# Singlets
## Briefs
## &
## Shorts

An Anthology of Poems from the *Show Me Shorts!*
*New Zealand Short Film Festival 2020*

**Edited by Trevor M. Landers**

Perehi o Mātātuhi Taranaki
Ngāmotu
2021

Published by PMT Press
In association with 99% Press,
an imprint of Lasavia Publishing Ltd.
Auckland, New Zealand
www.lasaviapublishing.com
2021

This book is copyright. Every Poem in this anthology is the intellectual property of the poet who wrote it. All images reproduced in this book are the intellectual property of Trevor M. Landers. Apart from any fair dealing for the purpose of private study, research, criticism or reviews, as permitted under the Copyright Act, no part of this book may be reproduced by any process without the permission of the publishers.

ISBN: 978-0-9951282-6-2

# Acknowledgments

I would like to thank the organisations that supported the creation of this book financially. Firstly the Franklin Local Board that have proudly and generously supported Poets from Franklin, Clarks Beach, Waiau Pa and Papakura District with a Creative Communities Grant. I would also like to thank New Plymouth District Council for supporting the inclusion of New Plymouth poets in this volume.

I would like to thank Gina Dellabarca for her support and collaboration. I would also like to thank Mike Johnson for his encouragement in creating this project and his offer to help publish. I would like acknowledge the genesis of this collection, a book in honour of the life of former New Zealand International Film Festival Director, Bill Gosden: *Whetu Mārama: Poems in Honour of Bill Gosden*, published by PMT Press in association with Plaistead Press, Palmerston North, (2021).

I am especially proud of, and would like to acknowledge, the many new poets who have found a voice in this anthology. Sponsoring the participation of emerging poets from Papakura and Taranaki has been especially satisfying. Conversely, the participation of established poets who have supported the approach and kaupapa of this volume has been immensely heartening.

Trevor M Landers

# Table of Contents

| | |
|---|---|
| 6 | Editorial Note: *Mike Johnson* |
| 7 | Foreword: *Gina Dellabarca* |
| 9 | Introduction: *Trevor M Landers* |
| 12 | The First Ever Film: *Trevor M Landers* |
| 105 | Contributers |

## The Sampler

| | |
|---|---|
| 16 | Ashmina, *Jacqueline Hogler* |
| 18 | Money Honey, *Mykaela Nyman* |
| 20 | Working Class, *Elvisa Van Der Leden* |
| 22 | David, *Katherine Joyce* |
| 24 | Super Comfort, *Trevor M Landers* |
| 26 | Mezze Stagioni, *Virginia Winder* |
| 28 | Frankie Jean & the Morning Star, *Gaenor Brown* |
| 30 | Every Other Summer, *Kristan Horne* |

## Aotearoa Online

| | |
|---|---|
| 34 | Oranges & Lemons, *Clare Erasmus* |
| 36 | Democracy, *Jeena Murphy* |
| 38 | We Rock, *Vira Paky* |
| 40 | Aitu, *Takunda Mazondiwa* |
| 42 | Aitu(a), *Katherine Joyce* |
| 43 | Biggie and Shrimp, *Francine Mula* |
| 44 | Zealandia, *essa may ranapiri* |
| 46 | Milk, *Trevor Landers* |

## International Time Zone Online

| | |
|---|---|
| 50 | The Explosion of a Swimming Ring, *Richard Von Sturmer* |
| 52 | Grab My Hand: A Letter to My Day, *Sierra Southam* |
| 54 | Tres Veces (Three Times), *Trevor M Landers* |
| 56 | Heading South, *Victor Billot* |
| 58 | The Watchmaker, *Ronnie Smart* |
| 60 | Cuckoo, *Arku Basu* |
| 62 | Kapaemahu, *Tu'u Lafelili'i* |

## UK Online

| | |
|---|---|
| 66 | My Brother is a Mermaid, *Vana Manasiades* |
| 68 | Just Agree Then, *Jordan Hamel* |
| 69 | The Fabric of You, *Rachel McAlpine* |
| 70 | Dungarees, *Lisette Prendé* |
| 72 | The Circle, *James Sagopotutele* |
| 74 | Talk Radio, *Trevor Landers* |
| 76 | Grandad was a Romantic, *Tim Jones* |
| 78 | Is This Free?, *Nod Ghosh* |

## Firm Favourites

| | |
|---|---|
| 84 | The $6.50 Man, *Selina Tusitala Marsh* |
| 86 | Noise Control, *Nick Ascroft* |
| 87 | Abiogenesis, *Richard Reeve* |
| 88 | Going to Mum's, *Michelle Elvy* |
| 92 | Just Like the Others, *Jack Ross* |
| 94 | Day Trip, *Trevor M Landers* |
| 96 | One Shoe Short, *Mercedes Webb-Pullman* |
| 98 | Koro's Medal, *Anton Blank* |
| 100 | Mokopuna, *Glenn Colquhoun* |
| 102 | The John, *Trevor M Landers* |

# Editorial Note

---

While much has been made, and justifiably so, of the devastating impact of Covid 19 on NZ tourism, the effect on the arts, particularly the performing arts, has been equally devastating. Poetry in performance has struggled, and films have been largely relegated to the small screen. In this environment, it seems right and natural that these two allied art forms should join forces in a book like this.

A short film is a visual poem. The shorter the film, the more it leans towards its literary sister form. Longer short films, say ten minutes or more, lean more towards the short story form. Both poetry and short films are marked by a concentration of imagery and a distillation of experience. They sit nicely side-by-side.

Engaging with this text is a fun, best enjoyed by watching the short films along with reading the poems. Together they make up a complete literary experience. 99% Press (Lasavia Publishing Ltd) is proud to be a part of this project, and I congratulate Trevor M Landers and Gina Dellabarca for bringing these poets and filmmakers together.

Mike Johnson, Editor of 99% Press

# Foreword: Gina Dellabarca

---

Tēnā koutou katoa. It is my pleasure to introduce a collection of New Zealand poetry inspired by short films. As the Festival Director of Aotearoa's leading international short film festival, *Show Me Shorts*, it gives me great joy to see how one art form can inspire another. Introducing a collection of poetry is not something I imagined I would be doing in 2020. In a year of turmoil, it is wonderful to be involved with a project that spreads thoughtful ideas and beautiful words that come from the heart. My thanks to Trevor Landers and all of the writers who have contributed work here.

Like the short films that give these poems their names, these are short stories distilled down to their essence. Reading them will inspire us to think more about our world, our identity and our potential. Many of the short films the poets have chosen can be viewed on our website, so I encourage you to check out the inspiration behind the words. I'm delighted that the writers include both new and emerging as well as established New Zealand poets. Fostering the careers of artists is a cause that benefits us all.

The way we consume artistic content of all kinds is evolving. In the film ecosystem that means cinema, theatre, TV, radio and digital are converging more closely. This collision is disrupting the media landscape and forcing adaptation. The momentum of change brings the opportunity to rethink the way we do things and can provoke artistic synergy. I hope to see more collaborations between artists of all types in the future, because I believe that fruitful collaboration and cross-fertilisation will result.

Tēnei te mihi nui ki ngā kaihanga kaituhi, mō rātou whakaaro, moemoeā, me wawata hoki. Our huge thanks to the writers, for their thoughts, dreams, and aspirations. Enjoy delving into the poems.

Gina Dellabarca, MNZM
Festival Director, Show Me Shorts Film Festival Trust

# Introduction

This ekphrastic anthology of poetry combines a love of poetry with a love of watching arthouse film. It was such an enjoyable experience I approached Gina Dellabarca, the *Show Me Shorts Film Festival* Director, to elicit her support for an anthology of poetry from a range of new, emerging and established poets. What follows is the manifestation of that single idea.

Each poem takes a single short film for its inspiration. The title of the poem is the same as the title of the short film, which served as its catalyst. The length, director and filming location are listed beneath the title. The collection does not require any familiarity with the films. The brief given to poets was to use the film as a spark for the imagination. Some have remained faithful to the plot lines and story arcs of their assigned short films, but most have used it as a springboard to somewhere completely different.

This collection is less about developing synergies between film and poetic texts, and more about a cross-fertilisation of art forms creating a bricolage. This mirrors the *Show Me Shorts* Festival: no one entry is similar to another and therefore we can confidently declare there is something for everyone.

Ekphrastic poetry is a popular poetry sub-genre, but what exactly is it? Ekphrastic poetry has come to be defined as poems written about works of art, however, in ancient Greece, the term ekphrasis was applied to the skill of describing a thing with vivid detail. Both meanings are in operation in this volume. Firstly, all of the poems were based, however directly, loosely or tangentially, on short films: the art form. Secondly, writers adopt an approach that encourages vividity, even if dreamy and amorphous.

In the first eight, *The Sampler,* the poets from Taranaki provide the lead, from the evoked nostalgia of Mykaela Nyman's poem to the conversational stylings of Van Der Leden. Between these are popular tropes (Brown), and the less familiar (Winder and myself). The second clutch looks at films from Aotearoa, showcasing many interesting themes, tangents and arcs while representing a diverse array of New Zealanders. I found the poems by Erasmus, Muzondiwa, Paky and Mula particularly intriguing, but all provide perspectives on what it means to be a New Zealander. This multiplicity of voices hints at a pluralistic future.

*The International Time Zone* gives this collection, depth, breadth and variety. Poets Basu, Billot and Lafelili'I piqued my interest. While I aim to capture the increasing internationalisation of poetry with my use of Spanish and Finnish.

The fourth clutch of Eight, *UK Online*, is another purse of amethysts, containing poems of sophistication, as well as notable experimentation, most obviously the notations and footnotes used by Manasiades. All poets in this section exhibit dexterity, imagination, nous and aplomb.

The final octet, *Firm Favorites*, features more established poets, like Ross, Reeve, Colquhoun and company, and provides the sweet *delice* to the degustation of the four 'course' banquet provided.

As a collection, these poems provide a kaleidoscopic view of modern life in New Zealand. They also show to some limited extent the interactions of a posse of New Zealand poets from all around the world united by their predilection for film. Often an appreciation of one art form leads to appreciation of others art forms. As writers and readers we do well to ensure our experiences are diverse and manifold and avoid becoming too anchored in the disciplines of poetry. In that way, both for readers and these poets, this volume represents refreshment.

Finally, this volume is best enjoyed as a bedside companion. Dip into just before bed, or as while on a blanket under the warm summer skies of Aotearoa. Enjoy!

Trevor M Landers, MA, MPM, MEd, MCW
Editor
Ngāmotu (New Plymouth)
July 2021

# The First Ever Short Film
*Trevor M Landers*

(i)
The font-head difficult to track to origin,
ten Lumière brothers' short films screened in Paris,
28 December 1895, Salon Indien du Grand Café, can
be regarded as the breakthrough of projected cinematographic motion pictures.
Though to be exact, in March 1885,
A Lumière Bros. film screening for 200 members of
the 'Society for the Development of the National Industry' was the first screening of a film with a sizeable audience.
Novelties then, now,
each less than a minute:
La Pêche aux poissons rouges, (Goldfish Fishers),
La Voltige (Horse Trick Riders),
Les Forgerons (Blacksmiths), and seven others,
would hardly draw a response of note.

(ii)
However the Lumières superseded:
shadowography,
the camera obscura,
shadow puppetry and magic lantern shows,
the phénakisticope, since 1832,
the zoetrope, since 1866,
Émile Reynaud›s Théâtre Optique,
Eadweard Muybridge's Zoopraxiscope,
Ottomar Anschütz's Electrotachyscope
Thomas Edison's Kinetoscope,
Kazimierz Prószyński's Pleograph,

Lauste and Latham's Eidoloscope
Max and Emil Skladanowsky's Bioscop,
Until 1927, no one would speak.

(iii)
Stories of light,
      the dance of image and shadow
          kindling of imaginations
     the promises of story-telling
       blazing across the screen
 seering retinas with new desires.

'Wines, Countdown Ostend, Waiheke Island',
Trevor Landers © 2020.
Please consume all alcohol responsibly.

The Sampler

# *Ashmina*

*15 mins, Dekel Berenson, Nepal/UK*
**Jacqueline Hogler**

Although it was a rainy cloudy windy morning
things are now completely crystal clear
torrential rain and winds
carry ideas to the clouds
seems no space to see the sky
low-lying thick blankets of elements
do not allow us to see
cumulonimbus clouds that fog a misty mind.
Though things are crystal clear
how do I know, how do I come to understand.
I wait patiently, marking seconds
fractured minutes to boil an egg with a black sand timer.
Things are completely crystal clear
everything is over very soon
one minute you're 13 then 63
what comes after
yes things are completely crystal clear
know how to wait

time quickly passes
watch the rainfall
watch the wind
See it move the branches of trees
limbs severed off by its abrupt kick
things are completely crystal clear
you hope
you hope to be able to hope
to be able to see you again
sometime this year
this month this week
before the storm
tomorrow maybe today
things will be as I've always wanted them to be
and not completely crystal clear.

# Money Honey

*10min, Isaac Knight-Wasbourne*
**Mikaela Nyman**

Black half-moons seize honeyed day

A girl with a heart
A boy with a toothbrush      life
         zipped
                 carried

80 cents won't buy an Elvis sandwich

Grab a fancy box of King cokes
bargain for Payday chocolates
find place            find    time
    find    skaters
the peckish take two at inflated prices

Not needing to think
         I only want a roof over my head

Not needing

She wishes she could wrap him up
(a melts-in-your-mouth-not-in-your-hand)
        keep him close    warm

But Kodak film has also gone out of fashion.

# Working Class

*10mins, Kyan Krumdieck, (NZ).*
**Elvisa Van der Leden**

"Follow your dreams," they said
"It'll be fun," they said
"What's your back up plan?" they said
"Be realistic" they said
"Be brave" I thought
"Be bold" I thought
"Why me?" I cried
"This is hard" I cried
"Be open" I learned
"Be patient" I learned
"You are worthy" I felt
"You are strong" I felt
"What do you do?" they asked
"How do you do it?" they asked
"Be humble" I thought
"Be considerate" I thought
"She is a good role model" I hoped
"She is genuine" I hoped

"Your dreams will change" I discovered
"It will be a journey" I discovered
"Be authentic. Be flexible. Be fearless. Be thoughtful.
Be Hopeful. Be kind." I repeat
As I live the dream of living.

# David

*12 mins, Zach Woods, (USA)*
**Katherine Joyce**

*David,*
*We wonder*
*If the thunder*
*is ever really going to begin, begin.*[1]

Happy man
sad man
life is a game everyone must play.

Suicidal man
euphoric man
even the mangy dog has its day.

Long days, dark days
life hanging by a thread
play the game.

---

*1 From the Morissey song 'National Front Disco', from the Your Arsenal Album.*

Spill your secrets
spill your guts
end up psychologically lame

No need to loop your rope
tomorrow may dawn again
so hold your head up high.

Discard the Citalopram
flush the Zopiclone
it far too sunny to die.

Hold off the psychotherapists
shoo away the faith healers
zealously guard your dime.

Spent the day in bed
leave the burdensome world behind

learn to cherish your own time.

# Super Comfort

*15 mins, Kirsikka Saari, (Finland).*
**Trevor Landers**


*Dynaamisella toiminnalla on sama kaikilla kielillä*
(Dysfuctionality is the same in every language)

    There is a gulf between them
  The closer she comes the further they gets
    The more she tries to please
        The more disgruntlement ensues.
There is no sailing in the luminous pools of midnight
    The ghostly galleons have long sailed off into the mystic,
  Super-comfort of daily negotiations.

*Toimintahäiriöstä voi tulla uusi alku*
(Out of dysfunction can come new beginnings)

    No matter how we came to be here;
whether by a love of the cinema,
    a University's miseducation,
  the gravitational pull of friend's suggestions,

a desire to think something new
or even the wish to find a place where we belong...
we are all family.
Within this group you will find mothers and fathers,
brothers and sisters, aunts and uncles, reconstituted afresh.

*Toimintahäiriöllä on yksi mukavuus*
(Dysfunction has its own comforts)

Small arms of a broken trees
cover multiple forms of covert abuses
even pleasantries can pierce the skin,
a dysfunctional family defined as
a family with more than one person in it.

# Mezze Stagioni
# (Transitional Seasons)

*10mins Riccardo Menicatti & Bruno Ugioli (Italy)*
**Virginia Winder**


Charon finds her twirling in sunlight
snatching at the air
crystal beads, whirling rainbows
over piano keys, along floorboards
across a timeline of books:
*'A Tree Grows in Brooklyn'*
*'Over My Dead Body'*
*'To Exodus'.*

Lydia,
He speaks quietly
as if rousing a sleepwalker

She's wide awake, at first light
bare feet soft on new Axminster
catching prisms, set in motion by sun fingers
magic windows, tentacled conifers, swaying
A cacophony of colour

Lydia,
It's time,
Take my hand.

Big brother
joins the game, they leap and grab bump and lunge
playing rainbows, spectrum triangles
slipping through kid velvet fists

Lydia,
Please,
We must go.

She looks up, curved mouth falls open
a vacant gape
Charon knows that moment
when a smile shifts from here to gone
Gently, he takes a sun-splotched hand
leads her over a river of memories
flying rainbows, dying with each step.

# *Frankie Jean & the Morning Star*

17 mins, Hannah Marshall, (NZ).
**Gaenor Brown**


She's pitched from all black night
passed to paddock's golden light
her forward steps in second phase
weave,                     swerve through damp dawn grass
Patterned play: win lose or draw, Bounce of the ball.
Ruck        Maul        Drive/ Rugby     is Life
Control the controllable, scrums, knock-ons ignored,
Kick, pressure into touch.
She's ever in training, ever in defence, rude calls
Injure       that no magic sponge can soothe.

But on the bridge up ahead
                a head is low.
She sees him- hunched in, his jersey, hoodie up-
padding against deep sorrow
This is dangerous play--to approach him
she's strapping up

             Strap up wāhine toa
You have an important conversion.
To make.

Silence the crowds            that diminish your soft
goodness
Win the crowds--there's no penalty here.
He's so far down in set piece play         fragmented
Exit play forming
The result weighs heavy
In these final moments      of extra time

Her mouth guard gone,
     she urges him    look for space    find    space
she dances him
back into the wind,
          play on into the morning sun.

# Every Other Summer

*6 mins, Christoph Green and Brendan Canty, (USA).*[2]

**Kristan Horne**

Someone on the fan site said
the lyrics are like, so depressing
And I thought to myself,
Well, exactly!

It is soothing
Initially, I liked him
because Jeff Tweedy puts into words
somethings I think but rarely articulate;
I like the words he uses.

Jeff's voice has just the right amount
Of Leonard Cohen-y throatiness
His voice has the gravel of Michael Stipe
He doesn't sound much like Jeff Buckley
But the lyrical snippets get stuck in your head.

---

2 *This poem is inspired by the short film 'Every Other Summer: The Covers' which is a companion piece to 'Every Other Summer', a 83 minute documentary about the Solid Sound Music Festival in North Adams, Massachussets, founded by Wilco.*

"You were right about the Stars,
each one is a setting sun"
His songwriting is genius
Because his imagery and metaphors are so beautiful
Even when he is "assassining down the avenue"
It sounds super-cool even if it is not easy to interpret.

My favourite album is hard to choose between
Yankee Hotel Foxtrot or A Ghost is Born
But YHF has the best songs on it,
And is a mix between the beautiful, sparse quieter ones
and the cacophonic, expansive ones,
but Summerteeth is good too.

One of my prized possessions is
photographs of me meeting Jeff Tweedy
at Wellington Airport, and the drumstick thrown into
the crowd at the Wellington Town Hall Concert.
Framed concert posters adorn the walls of my home
I vehemently deny I am obsessed.

'Harakeke, Waiheke Island', Trevor Landers © 2020

# 2

# Aotearoa Online

# *Oranges and Lemons*

*13 mins, Robyn Grace, (New Zealand).*
**Clare Erasmus**

The sweetness of sunlight brushes her youthful skin,
skipping through the meadows in juvenile delight
whimsical thoughts,
nature's euphoria,
Fills up her soul,
with smiles of flowers,
greetings of telling tussock
fresh country air perfumes her heart.

Deep in the dark woods,
a feral possum awaits,
like a villain preparing with rancid intent
to plunder
to ransack
her joyful enchantment of utter bliss
drips of the toxicity
she skips right by.

Iridescent is the night sky,
bright in its beauty,
smiling sweet thoughts on her innocent heart,
wonders of hope,
kisses of love
acceptance,
serenity of youthfulness,
she saps up the nectar of purity.

# Democracy

*14 mins, Finnius Tippett, (New Zealand).*
**Jeena Murphy**

Len's truth marches on
propelled outwards from home
by the ballot box

Dad's up for re-election
his opposition's fierce
controversial policies on pasta and frittata
sink him faster than white water rafters.

Out campaigned by Mary
cake and voter bribes.
electoral fraud, nothing to applaud,
ballot tampering's so fracturing.

In with New Dad, Mary
out with Old Dad, Len
family roles re-engineered;
keep the voters calm.

Mary's truth marches on
to the thrum and boom of brass
all power to the ballot box
pay homage to family democracy.

# We Rock

*13 mins, Morgan Leary, (New Zealand)*
**Vira Paky**

it begins with that drumbeat
trickling in from an open window
sparks ignite across my chest
yet, a body like this lies in limbo
too full, too much rolling hips, too loud
no room for a voice so soft to billow
always drowned in sea of condemnation
not a home of yours to breathe, they say
their sharp words echo in my skull

remain behind them, remember your place
remain behind them, remember your place
remain behind them, remember your place

hushing myself into nothing
tearfully whispering into the cracks
but the feeling will not relax
growing too strong to resist
each moment, longing to brisk

desperate to move, being bond by virile rope
knots dig into the flesh, shattering hope

until i am home among this melodious bevy
here, my chest flutters full
once glaring eyes, now watchful and warm
finally, this body can twist and turn
this quiet voice, now weighted and firm
every note incurs praise and affirmation
fullness and richness lie in every wake

the rhythm begins to flow like a river
overflowing, rushing and babbling
kind cheers and laughter dispel any unbeliever
every thick gravitated coil begins to shake
head thrown back; eyes tightly clasped
rolling my shoulders, winding the hips
throating vibrating, climbing up every decibel
like a ship that will not stop rocking

and we rock on and on and on...

# Aitu

*7 mins, Piripi Curtis, and Gabrielle Faaiuaso,*
*(New Zealand)*
**Takunda Muzondiwa**

Everything that goes up must come down
so we stopped gods from floating in the sky
deflated the clouds
vacuum cleared the stars
milked galaxies into black holes
because we're all mortal
afraid of what that means
we call gods to live among us.
Hoping their presence will be infused into the air we
breathe, fuelling our sense of grandiosity
we're fragile and brittle with an indestructibility
complex, all talk with no conviction
all walk with no backbone
even the soil listens to the cartilage between our toes
croak in fear with each stride.
We told gods to live here so we could mimic them
better
we made gods run on clockwork
every day is a workday we spend shadowing them

swallowing them.
If humans can't be gods
we'll consume everything godly
until our destruction looks holy
let's flood continents and call it genesis
set lands ablaze and call it a testimonial climax
rob gods from the sky and call it rebirth
If everything that goes up must come down
What happens when those below start believing they
are above all else? Who will tell them only gods belong
above?
Aitu
Aitu
Aitu
We are all mortal
the destruction we create in trying to forget that
will always remind us
*Ātua belong to the skies,*
we have always belonged to the ātua.

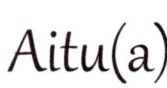

# Aitu(a)

*7 mins, Piripi Curtis and Gabrielle Faaiuaso, (New Zealand)*
**Katherine Joyce**


Into the ink of night
the car was a nib
bit of a clapped out old banger
the sound of a pakaru exhaust pipe
arriving before it did, then the palls of blue smoke.

That night,
they raced past Hutton's paddock,
near the dip in the road after Mrs Imlah's place
not noticing the squad car behind them
The dazzling lights lighting up the night like a carnival.

Ānei i te aitua
Ānei i te whakaari mariko
Ānei i te tipua rerekē
Nō muri mai, ka kitea ko te tino anahera tonu
Tō tāua motokā pākaru te tero o te tīkaokao.

# Biggie and Shrimp

*14 mins, Harvey Hayes, New Zealand*
**Francine Mula**

As they light him a cigarette
he loses another battle.
On his darkest nights,
the shepherd forsakes the cattle.

Warmth he craves,
in his never-ending days.
A thousand miles to go
before he finds his way home.

A single step
Is better than an in-place jog.
Hapless is the man who attempts to swim,
While another wishes him to drown.[3]

---

[3] *Author's note: I was inspired by the internal and external conflicts such as their living situation and identity-wise conflicts that the protagonist experiences in the film. You can see how he tries to pick himself up every day but is diverted by his unruly neighbour and unstable family relationships instead. I found this as to be the key idea in the film because like Biggie, we struggle daily to fight our inner and/ or outer turmoil in our everyday lives.*

# Zealandia

*15 mins, Bruno de Bruin, (New Zealand).*
**essa may ranapiri**

    i caught                  something
    i             caught
    a border
    i crushed       my     self
                        into a state

         we only exist
       thank you stolen
land
thank
you stolen land
 now
      shares name w/     white supremacist
movement + a wildlife
     a wild / life                 sanctuary

alpha      only exists in a
prison
artificial     dynamics

a family playing
mono           poly
      or the land lords           game
a snake           stretching out
on a        deck chair
eat ur apple and die!

shares whakapapa w/ history of
white        ness        ness     in
a lake        so sick        not like
dude that        is sick        but like
dying           dying as in dead     already
      i press my tongue into
the holes of a gas mask       and
laugh and laugh and laugh
there are so many ways of
getting over it

              none of them involve
just waiting.

# Milk

*14 mins, Pennie Hunt, (2020).*
**Trevor Landers**


The miasma of seaborne fog
descending like a dampened blanket
on improbable historical fact
a submarine loitering off the coast of Otago
for a pail of fresh cow's milk.

Ich bin vor der Küste herumlungern
Ich wollte einen Milchshake
Es wird durstig auf einem U-Boot
Wirgingen an Land, um eine Kuh zu plündern.
Die macht der deutschen Kriegsmarine.

Does this mean there might be a Russian nuclear sub
moored silently off the coast of Oamaru,
waiting for the Black Friday sales to begin
snaffling 59-inch televisions
and other valuable consumer goods?

Возможно нет.
Надеюсь, что нет.

The Sea Floor just offshore, North Mariana Islands,
© Trevor Landers, (2018).

# 3

## International Time Zone Online

# The Explosion of a Swimming Ring

*10 min, Tommi Setajoki, (Finland).*
**Richard Von Sturmer**


Granddad's sipping his lemonade
in the spa pool
with a sprig of mint
at five past four
in the afternoon.

How often do they change the water?
And the lemonade?
Is it freshly squeezed
or kept in green bottles
dug up from the bottom of the sea?

There's a patterning of ripples
after someone slices
into the big pool—
little tents of waves
each like the blue umbrella
you drop into your glass.

Did you hear that?
A jet fighter passed overhead
shattering the sound barrier.

Looking down
you see that you've cut your thumb.
Blood corpuscles spill out
the size of donuts.
You shiver.
Alice wears her water wings.
It's still five past four
in the afternoon.

# Grab My Hand: A Letter to My Dad

*Camrus Johnson, USA (2020).*
**Sierra Southam**

Grab my hand.
Fingers interlocking.
Let me show you something.

Follow me
just this once,
just the two of us,
just follow me -
as we hollow out a space
between the memories.

Grab my hand and let me show you
the child that aches to know you.
She's buried in here, somewhere.
I hear her sometimes.
She claws her way to the surface,
hungry for you.
I'd like you to meet me.

In between the memories,
where time flows backwards,
we backtrack to times
where the future doesn't matter,
where we live for every moment,
for the un-laughed laughter,
where we forgive each other,
and grow up together.

Grab my hand, and tell me
it'll be okay
instead of fading away.
And hey -
maybe now
we can mean the things we say.

So grab my hand.
Fingers interlocking.
Discovering something
in the space between the memories.

# Tres Veces (Three Times)

*20 mins, Spain, (2019).*
**Trevor M Landers**

Three times
The cock crowed
Three times
The cock rose

*Tres Veces*
*El gallo cantó*
*Tres veces*
*El gallo se levantó*

The centurion raises his sword
& loses his ear
another young trojan disfigured.

*El centurión levanta su espada*
*y pierde la oreja*
*otro joven troyano enculado*

perfidy, blasphemy, buggery & treachery
Is this a defence of religion, a bulwark, a bastion?
*Perfidia, blasfemia, sodomía y traición.*

Hidden shadows lie in wait
stalking its prey, seeking a warm vulnerability,
charity and kindness, can this be your undoing?
Remember, one Crocodile is always ready to pounce

*Depredadores ocultos acechan*
*acechando a su presa,*
*buscando una vulnerabilidad*
*¡Siempre* hay *un cocodrilo listo para saltar!*

I acknowledge you
I absolve of you
Your infractions are forgiven
Run man! Leave here!
I give you absolute forgiveness
It is what we always do.

# Heading South

*12 mins, Yuan Yuan, (USA/China).*
**Victor Billot**

Nothing is ever the same.
Spiralling out into space
from where you've come.

Things break down:
every step leads you away.

Maybe it wasn't so great,
from where you came, anyway.
When things are broken,
they don't always set straight.
Survival and love
are never close friends.

This world spins too fast.
The skin we were given too thin.
Nothing remains. Not the same.

# The Watchmaker (Mockumentary)

*5 mins, Charlie Fonville, USA, (2019).*
**Ronnie Smart**

*(St. Bede, in 'The Ecclesiastical History of the English People,' compared the brevity of human life to that of a sparrow passing at winter through a warm mead hall and then back into winter.)*

As clock hands fly across their face
or minutes torture in their roles,
a bird flies through the marketplace.

When projects topple from their base
or fail to follow or control
the clock, hands shake. On the face

of it, all things have left their places,
but when you see a new-born foal,
a bird flying through the marketplace,
or feel a partner's warm embrace,
this chase of time is an empty goal.

Then clock hands fly across their face,
time drops a second out of place,
you try to question this whole
'Bird flying through the marketplace'
kind of life, but the race of hours wears you down.

Time tolls, the clock hands fly.
Past your face,
a bird flies through the marketplace.

# Cuckoo

*7 mins, Jörgen Scholtens, The Netherlands*
**Arku Basu**

Cuckoo! Cuckoo!
Time rages in ticks and bounds
off the mind's easel and into the reel,
always on track but behind
the eyes that lock on to the hands of god.
Cuckoo! Cuckoo!
What becomes of it when it is gone,
when it is past, packaged, and outmoded
as memory?
Who keeps it?
Who loses it?
Are we all timekeepers,
tied to our seats,
hostage to a unceasing train of images?
Cuckoo! Meow!
Is that the sound of the moment—passing?
Cuckoo! Cuckoo!
Is that an omen, a portent, amassing
in the corners of your dream,

as you sleep like a baby, again.
Cuckoo! Cuckoo!
It is time
waiting for you,
loyally, devoted to its own being
as well as yours,
until you stop counting
and the world erupts
in silence.

# Kapaemahu

*9 mins, Hinaleimoana Wong-Kalu, Dean Hamer, and Joe Wilson, (Hawai'i).*
**Tu'u Lafealeli'i**

*A oia mau malihini he u'i kanaka leo mali'u, a he nonohe waipahe no na'e.* (The visitors were tall and deep in voice, yet gentle and soft-spoken).

*Ua fa'aalia e Kapaemahu le malosi fa'amalolo o ma'a uiga ese e fa i luga o le matafaga o Waikiki - ma agaga lauiloa o lo'o i totonu o latou tino.*

*I aso la ua leva, e to'afa tagata ta'itasi o itulua male male fafine agaga na aumaia le fa'amalologa mai Tahiti i Hawaii. O le igoa o le latou ta'ita'i o Kapaemahu.*

*Alofagia e tagata mo o latou auala agamalu ma fa'amalologa faavavega, na latou totoina ai ni maa tetele se fa ma o latou malosiaga. O ma'a o lo'o tu pea i luga o le mea ua ta'ua nei o Waikiki Beach, ae o le tala moni i tua atu o latou na natia - e o'o mai i le taimi nei.*

*O Kapaemahu na te toe fa'aleleia lenei tala fa'asolopito i se olaga olaola, e va'aia e mata o se tamaititi fiailoa.*

*Aua e le lava e a'oa'o ai la matou gagana i se
potua'oga, pe faitau e uiga i la matou tala'aga i se tusi
Igilisi gagana. E mana'omia ona tatou toaaga i le
fa'amatalaina o a tatou tala ia tatou lava ala.
Fa'amalo atu ia te oe i sea ituaiga tala maoa'e!*

**Rough translation**

Kapaemahu reveals the healing power of four mysterious stones on Waikiki Beach and the legendary transgender spirits within them. Beloved by the people for their gentle ways and miraculous cures, they imbued four giant boulders with their powers. The stones still stand on what is now Waikiki Beach. Such stories need to be told by mahu, third-gender people, reclaimed from colonial censorship and overlay, in our own languages.

'Westminister Streetscene', Trevor Landers © 1997

#  ৫

## UK Online

# My Brother is a Mermaid

*20 mins, Alfie Dale, (UK)*
**Vana Manasiades**

Dogfish: Thessalonike[4] responds to critics:
Not bird   not alien   not beaked not winged
not washed   not chorused   not unmeshed   not dogfish
not creatured   not kelp   not diving   not saline
Not headfirst   not witnessed   not unless

Yes,   bird[5]
yes,   alien[6]
yes,   beaked[7]
yes,   winged [8]
yes,   washed[9]
yes,   chorused[10]
yes,   unmeshed[11]
yes,   dogfish[12]

---

*4 famous mermaid*
*5 rachis for fingers*
*6 glands for longing*
*7 tongue for tasting*
*8 like monsters*
*9 like coral*
*10 like countries*
*11 and unlocked*
*12 and glass skinned*

| | | |
|---|---|---|
| yes, | creatured | [13] |
| yes, | kept[14] | |
| yes, | diving[15] | |
| yes, | saline[16] | |
| *yes,* | *headfirst[17]* | |
| *yes,* | *witnessed[18]* | |

---

*13 ναι, σκυλόψαρο*
*14 above the driftwood*
*15 through sleek returning*
*16 against your side*
*17 against the grasses*
*18 my seahorses roped to spinifex*

# Just Agree Then

*7 minutes, Duncan Cowles and Ross Hogg, (UK).*
**Jordan Hamel**


shoot for images / cut for narrative later / it will find you / slipping through neglected fields / like a serpent / mouse / child / climbing a tree trunk / leg / something / write for narrative / cut for menace / beauty / amber in the bark / later / check the framing on that / it will find you / like a maverick process server / serving their own / process first / plough / sow / burn / the field / later / watch creatures scaled / feathered / rust slip out of frame / pull focus / context comes / later / follow the escape / not the scorched roots / check the scarring on that / plan for every living thing / who saw it differently / cut together / find / take / leave / the parts of this poem you want / in the field / cut / pull / burn the rest / later

# The Fabric of You

*11 mins, Josephine Lohoar Self, UK, (2019).*
**Rachel McAlpine**

A wall of jackets amplifies
your voice of jagged silk.
My tiny pain. My lost.

I built such oh such
a moat of pins and threads
interwoven, overlocked.

I was tweed I was wrong.
This my ever-ever song:
only a tiny tailor
never a brave little king.

# Dungarees

*6 mins, Abel Rubinstein, UK, (2020).*
**Lisette Prendé**


Beneath
chipped nail polish,
Beneath,
Him or Her or They,
Beneath
Son/Daughter
Sister/Brother,
O' lover,
we reside.

Beneath skin,
hair,
cells
DNA.

We are energy.
Particles in a dance.
Like attracts like,
drawing me to you.

Who needs costumes when you're not playing pretend?

You lean in,
stroke my cheek,
offer an eyelash and say
"Make a wish."

My breath across your fingers.
Your laugh like summer.
"I see you" you say,
with a playful smile.
Eyes as blue as dungarees.

# The Circle

*16 mins, Lanre Malaolu, UK, (2019).*
**James Sagapolutele**

*David & Sanchez, uso uli,*
*Le toe fa'apogisaina e East London igoa tauleleia*
*gaioiga fa'atonutonu, valivali se ata*
*se tapoleni o tamaloloa,*
*le fa'afaigofieina o le soifua maloloina o le*
*mafaufau, fa'ailoga masani.*
*Seti i se poloka tenement,*
*luga o se tofi o le taulaga i totonu o le taulaga,*
*fou auala i tala.*
*Vaelua le pupuni, gaioiga & fa'atalanoaga*
*vali-o-numera & olaga moni.*
*Le o le masani, soona fai tala*
*le to'afilemu, talavou uli tau'oloa tuputupu ae*
*e le o le le mautonu, ae tumu i le malosi o le*
*talavou, malosi'a fusi aiga ma le fealofani,*
*pei o ii: Pāpākura, Pāpātoetoe, Otāhūhū*
*o nofoaga nei e le o ni graneneta.*

David & Sanchez, brothers black,
Not blackened further by East London reputations,
bold directorial movements,
painting a portrait, a canvas of masculinities,
the easement of mental health, familiar stigmas.
Set in a tenement block,
on an inner city council estate,
innovative approach to storytelling.
Divide the screen, movement & interview
choreography & real life---a dialogic conversation.
Gone are the usual, hackneyed stories
underprivileged, young black men growing up,
further reject the unrelentingly grim,
full of youthful energy, strong family ties and
camaraderie, just like here: Pāpākura, Pāpātoetoe,
Otāhūhū are places not grenades.[19]

---

*19 English translation edited and 'spritzed' for poetic effect with the permission of the author.*

# Talk Radio

*9 mins, Ben S Hyland, UK, (2019).*
**Trevor Landers**

I am haunted:
not by poltergeists
or earthly apparitions
but by my unlived lives.
These parallel universes
won't ever speak,
they took an oath
to keep their truths from me
ringing talkback radio
at absurd hours of the night.

I have words and voices
humming in my head
chirruping like lost frequencies
that will never be met
outside of my bed.
I have to accept
I cannot have it all,
I have to accept
knowing nothing, or I know something.

I have been haunted by hubris
in the small wee hours
listened to all kinds of narrow-minded contempt
& manifold forms of insomnia
posing as wisdom and experience
it seems that prejudice does not sleep either.

I am a 'first time caller'
summoning courage to articulate a point
the romance of the airwaves
the solemnity of another love-lorn night
I am ruler of this dominion, momentarily,
harnessing the power of the radio:
Now, you are talking!
Hello, Jeremey, well I believe in the elimination of
poverty but your last caller...

# Grandad Was A Romantic

*5 mins, Maryam Mohajer, UK, (2019).*
**Tim Jones**

Grimsby docks after all these years
seagulls, oil slicks and Brexiteers
a ghost trawler, a skeleton crew
Grandad, the romance is pretty much through.

Here I stand in Freeman Street
fag packets, skag, and Uber Eats
The fish are gone and the jobs gone too
Grandad, the romance is pretty much through.

In your day the seas ran red with cod
boon of a stern but benevolent God
You over-fished and then blamed the EU
Grandad, the romance is pretty much through.

You wanted my father close to your side
He sailed instead on the post-war tide
To colonised lands with construction to do
Grandad, the romance is pretty much through.

It took me fifty years to return
With my unshed tears, my father's urn
To the city that kept its hold over you
Grandad, the romance is pretty much through.

A freezing wind, a cold grey shore
I head for my cousins, who unbolt their doors
Tell family stories until they come true
Grandad, the romance is not yet quite through.

# Is This Free?

*12 mins, UK, Lauris Benerts*
**Nod Ghosh**

*Is this free?* she asks
and because I have
often thought about
miscommunication
I ask her about
the possibility of snow
the chance we will be
together live long and
die in each other's arms
the moment is fleeting
because I only ask her
with my eyes and
then she is gone

*Is this free?* you ask
and I hesitate
....
for everything
has a price I say
to agitate you

I lie, when you
place your
metaphorical tongue
on mine, and taste
my acid discomfort

*Is this free?* he asks
because even privilege
has its price
*Is this free? Is this free?*
it costs me nothing to
tell him to fuck off

*Is this free?*
I'll interrogate every stereotype
and extract an answer
from below your
uncomfortable collar
your mouth will say no
though I'll want it to say yes

*Is this free?*
I inflicted unseen
paranoia on her
my newspaper eyes
cold unlit spies
when she asked
*Is this free, Is this free,*
*Is this free?* I did nothing
to dispel her doubts
and then she was gone

*Is this free?* you ask
I request your help
don't need your answers
I only want you
to acquiesce and
yet you reply
so pleasantly
before you guess my
disingenuous game

*Is this free?*
you, the man who says no
will return
*Is this free? Is this free?*
you won't look
as if you lived
a holocaust
you'll have
the eyes of someone
who'll travel time
asking
*Is this free? Is this free?*

*Is this free?*
he wouldn't let her have the chair
he knew there was nobody there
he made a joke to disconcert her
hoping she would go elsewhere
but *Is this free?* she asked again
and he felt her ever growing pain
and let the woman have his seat
filled the space between them
with wild conjecture and deceit

*Is this free?*
you'll ask again
and I'll drown in
the ambiguity of your thoughts
what might I discern
through the lens of your eyes
your hands, your ears
the depth of your unease
your sinews, your face
and you'll ask once more
*Is this free? Is this free?*
I'll question you until
I trick you into silence

'Angel and Paisley 'helping' with the washing'.
Trevor Landers © 2020

# 5

# Firm Favourites

# The Six Dollar Fifty Man

*Mark Albiston and Louis Sutherland 15 mins, (2009).*
**Selena Tusitala Marsh**

Fly, fly
As fast as you can
You can't catch me
I'm the $6.50 man
     Red sun bullies
     Their kryptonite slurs
     Drain me of power
     Rob me of words
To them difference is unholy
I'm too outta the box
They try to control me
Fill my pocket with rocks
     And if I believe it
     If I think it's true
     I'm blind to my beauty
     I'm blind to you
But my red line is the read line
I write my own myth
I peel the skin of myself
Swallow pit and pith

                    I see the red school roof
                    I climb to the top
                    Cape slung behind
                    There's nothing to stop
Me from jumping to death
But instead, in belief
I fly through the air
Body, soul, mind free
                    I fly into the infinite
                    Yellow sun galaxy
                    It burns bright
                    With my possibilities
I land on the earth
Without injury
I walk away
A priceless me.

# Noise Control

*Phil Simmonds, 10 mins (2008)*
**Nick Ascroft**

A capon is, according to the Oxford,
a castrated cock – a rooster – fattened
for the eating. Not aware the cocks had
had this done, we ate a couple, that, and
they were quite delectable, our – what
exactly? I suppose – our squeamishness? –
well, probably not mattering a jot.

And on encountering the heinousness
of prog that blasted out the front-room curtain
of the neighbour's cottage down the bank,
the word returned to mind. And I made certain
if not capon cock rock now, the shank
would come. I called the council on the band.
'Yeah no they're not too loud,' I said, 'too bland.'

# Abiogenesis

*5 mins, Richard Mans, USA, (2011).*
**Richard Reeve**

Circuit,
in the back blocks

of thought,
dust spinning

along a dry bed,
observe yourself—

a region,
a fragment,

hairy fire,
assuming

in the core
of a mountain

the dreams
of ghosts.

# Going to Mum's

*Lauren Jackson, 13 mins, (2013).*
**Michelle Elvy**

be patient
>when weather is stormy
>when people are stormy
>when you step in the puddle
>when you can't finish the puzzle
>when you –
>when you –

be patient
>the noise is loud, this to-ing and fro-ing
>the bustling and shouting
>the coming and going
>between this place and that
>this thought and that
>this moment and that

be patient
> pull on your layers, your armour
> pull on long sleeves, long pants, thick-soled shoes
> you'll need them all some days
> but listen to the quiet in your chest and

be patient
> winter is cold
> you need to wait out
> forces of nature

be patient
> snug your cap
> wrap your scarf
> button your puffer

be patient
> and when spring comes and you
> peel back the layers, one by one,
> feel the light shine
> slant through your blinds
> see the crocus smile
> at the world

be patient
> listen
> and ask for help

when you're going to Dad's
> hold the ladder when he climbs
> to clear shelves, to reach spaces too high
> finish the puzzle you started in July
> see his smile? it's for you,
> it's nourishment

when you're going to Mum's
> jump the puddle left by spring showers
> find her out back and kneel down
> next to her, hand her the trowel
> she can't reach, the seeds from the packet,
> put your fingers in the soil of her garden, and
> dig deep

# Just Like the Others

*Jackie van Beek, 10 mins, New Zealand, (2009).*
**Jack Ross**

All you have to learn
is how to be alone

my Dad wrote Admit nothing
in his diary

in the retirement home
I used to duck inside

the library at school
to foil the wolfpacks

go undercover
if your earbuds

secretly connect
to nothing

broadcasting silence
smile   disguise it

with a whistle
eventually you'll find

the one who shows
the sign you need

received and understood

# Day Trip

*Zoe McIntosh, 11 minutes, (2010).*
**Trevor Landers**


Freedom's sweet undertow
    allure foaming in wave-wash
        compulsions of forward movement
  the traveller's idyll:
                'round the next bend,
              over the next hill,
          across the next border,
    there we shall find ourselves without
    discombobulation,
           exalted to our highest plane.

Skin-deep tethering
        to the inescapable self,
    victories of psychotherapy seemingly annulled
        the moko, a leather jacket
Mangare Mapu, Te Rohe Pōtae, 4 eva,
    do we ever leave? Will they allow us
        fresh beginnings, a new day's rapture?
    to have adventures, as intrepid daytrippers

together, be it:
 Picton, Cinque Terre, Mo'orea, Santorini, Venezia,
Hjørundfjord, Khasab, Fort-de-France, Kotor, Juneau
or Capetown.
    Shall we go together?Have we been already?

Friend, reason shall be the reformation of deaf ears,
    poetry sent forth to melt a hardening heart
like quelling a querulous child,
        or to woo soft breasts to wonderment.
Pay no heed to the panjandrums of style & verse
    garlanded in emptiness and Narcissus
backing the latest jester without keenness of eye
    euphonious, giddy brashness all the same,
e hoa, let your heart chart its own tremulous course,
    & have the courage to swim after it.

# *One Shoe Short*

*Jackie van Beek, 8 mins, New Zealand, (2008).*
**Mercedes Webb-Pullman**

A jumbled case of shoes
unpaired, none fit
to go to school
                        Jesse waits for me
                            we're still a pair
                  but the bus leaves on schedule
I run out of my borrowed shoes
before the bridge
my toes dance under the seat
                            engine and tires
                    drone like music made with
                      sunshine, voices and sticks
will my lessons run
out through my soles
if I don't wear shoes?
                will they fly through the camp
                like scraps, like dust through
                fences made of holes?

school door groans and closes
moans and closes on me
left out, left outside.
      Jesse and I fight for my place
       we try a shoe for him a shoe for me
         the door shuts on us both
off to giggle in the Mall,
cold air in the butchers
sausages not steak for Aunty
        so Jesse can buy me new shoes
         pink as a mob of galahs
         morning-sky sparkling
I'd like slippers made of feathers
to take back over the bridge
not plastic
        they hobble me, I stumble
       can't race, can't kick a football in them
          can they fly?

# Koro's Medal

*James Barr, 14 mins, New Zealand, (2011).*
**Anton Blank**

Keri had had an inkling when she was pregnant that he wouldn't be like the other boys. Or was it the psychic, what had he said again? An unusual child, that's right he'd said yes, you'll definitely have a child, only one, there's something different about them. I feel their presence, they're not far off, he's saying he wants to comfort you. God knows I need the comfort, Keri said, uncles and aunts dying with alarming regularity, the passing of the dynasty, a handful of beige grandchildren forced into the front row of rituals that made them feel uncomfortable, poorly equipped. It's like sitting behind the soldiers, Keri thought as she shifted from side to side on the hard wooden-bench. She liked watching the faces on the other side, staring into the middle-distance, polar-fleece sweaters zipped into their chins. Nodding off. Words hanging like lobes. The nothingness of it all, the boredom and displacement. The collision. Keri was determined to go it alone, the fertility treatment, the anonymity all flying in the face of heavily laden expectations. She attended the necessary gatherings, volumes of bright-pink fabric billowing to accommodate her belly. Keri could feel the latent disapproval she'd experienced since childhood. But she didn't give a fuck, not in a belligerent way, Keri just didn't care what other people thought of her. Her Australian PA said you're just a square peg luv, a square peg in a round hole, as she cackled like a kookaburra. Like what the fuck is the child going to be like? Not like the other boys, Keri said, he won't be like the other boys. The father's a homosexual for starters. Who'd have thought back in the day that you'd be able to get pregnant without having sex? shouted the Australian. Keri has a charcoal sketch by a well-known Māori artist; a tiny foetus at the centre of a koru, emerging out of the blackness. Hawaiki, the place we come from and return to, the aunts and uncles are in transit. Poor, sweet baby, make your way home, Keri whispers. Watching him play, she knows he's not interested, he's indifferent to the excitable boys in the sandpit. He's sitting on the edge of the wooden box that defines the perimeter, picking the petals off the daisies he's plucked from the grass. Smiling at Keri on the bench he holds a stalk skyward, triumphant. Te Rā, Keri had wanted a Māori name that was easy to pronounce, nothing that could be bastardised. She thought about teachers in classrooms chocked full of children calling out Te Rā, Te Rā, the sun, the sun! An exhortation! The hope! The beauty! As he grew older, the differences became more pronounced, the awkwardness, the unbearable challenge of just being. I don't want to wear the clothes, I don't want to play the sport, I don't want to be part of it, I don't fit in. Te Rā weeps; a tall willowy adolescent, delicate, angular. His tribe will find him eventually; sitting amongst them Te Rā's insouciance for the conventional life will be entirely logical. Keri's anxiety will pass, she will know that the change has been entirely necessary. The whānau will creak and groan under the pressure of external forces and the scorching heat of the sun.

# Mokopuna

*Ainsley Gardiner, 11 mins, New Zealand, (2009).*
**Glenn Colquhoun**

This river is
swift and deep.
See how its
fists curl.
It keeps itself to itself.
This river mutters.

Blah. Blah. Blah.
Te mea. Te mea.
Te mea. Te mea.

Where both of them
meet it is hard to know
when one turns
into the other.

Slips and slurs.
Fists and words.
Twists and turns.

Some call this trouble.
Some call this having-a-crack.
Some call this raruraru.
I call it love.

In time they
will come
to the sea.

Ten thousand secrets
whisper there.
I will remember
every drop of them
as they return
and wash me
clean away.

# The John

*12 mins, Neil Sonnekus, South Africa/New Zealand, (2015).*
**Trevor Landers**

*Duitsers het die bloed van die Holocaust*
  *en die finale oplossing op hul hande,*
*die wit Suid-Afrikaner, die stank van apartheid,*
  *ongeag die skuld.*

Top of Karangahape Road
  a seedy dive bar putrefacting in the gloom,
  among strip clubs, indifferent art galleries
    and the pointless hubbub of commuter traffic
  this dingey place, magnet for afternoon loners
watering hole of wilderbeest, injured antelopes
    tended by a visibly invisible Asian: Trix,
      jarring a level of accountability;
    two jettisoned lovers,
  the engineer and the actor
    in aftermath, shards of relationships gone west,
      grappling with the aetiology of ethnocentricity,
        between witty banter,
      a chauvinism and bitterness spilling forth

a desire for straight-shooting, bullet-candour
the disestablished, the freshly discarded
  their misguided attempts at solidarity and succour
  the animus & venom
             just beneath the surface,
         sneering contemptibility with pistolette
   things steadily going down the toilet,
       talking past each other, pissing spite.

*Stel ,n fokken dom vraag,*
        *wie sal jy ondersteun as die Bokke die All Blacks speel?*
*Onbelangrik.*
        *Maak nie saak nie, die gemiddelde Japie of Kiwi is so*
*asinien soos die ander.*
            *Verken die verskille!*

# Contributers

**Nick Ascroft** is the author of four collections of poetry from Victoria University Press. The most recent, *Moral Sloth* (2019), sides with the scumbag majority who want the world to be changed around them with minimum inconvenience. Nick sprang up out of the earth in Oamaru and is sliding back down into it in a government job in Wellington.

**Arku Basu** is pursuing a PhD in English at the University of Auckland. His research focuses on the presence of 'erotic space' in the early and middle works of Iris Murdoch. Usually, he forgets to wear his watch, which results in mostly good days when he spends less time looking at his watch and being more productive.

**Victor Billot** was born in Dunedin in 1972. In 2020 he was commissioned by the Newsroom website to write a series of political satires in verse. His poems have been displayed in the Reykjavik City Hall and in Antarctica. His collection, *The Sets*, will be published by Otago University Press in early 2021.

**Anton Blank** (Ngāti Porou/Ngāti Kahungunu) is a child advocate, communications consultant, writer and editor who lives in Auckland. Over a twenty-
five-year career Anton has worked across a broad range of areas focused on Maori development. He is founder and editor of the Maori literary journal *Ora Nui*.

**Gaenor Brown** is a teacher, actor, director and dramaturg at WordSpark Applied Theatre and Drama in New Plymouth. She lectures in the Faculty of Education at the University of Waikato and is currently completing a practice-led PhD exploring the notion of belonging in the applied theatre ensemble. Words create transformational images for sharing, performing - hence her delight in all poetry.

**Glenn Colquhoun** is a poet and GP who works in Horowhenua. He was born in 1964 and grew up in South Auckland. He studied theology for two years at Avondale College in Australia and completed a BA in English and Education at Auckland University in 1987. He later attended Auckland Medical School, graduating in 1996.

**Michelle Elvy** lives in Ōtepoti Dunedin. She edits at *Flash Frontier: An Adventure in Short Fiction* and is Reviews Editor for *Landfall*. Recent collaborations include Ko Aotearoa Tātou | We Are New Zealand (OUP, 2020) and Love in the Time of COVID: A Chronicle of a Pandemic, curated with Witi Ihimaera. Her book include *the everrumble* and *the other side of better*.

**Clare Erasmus** is an author and poet living in the city of Christchurch. She has written books for both educators and children. Clare works full time as a local teacher and spends much of her free time writing and studying towards her PhD in Education.

**Nod Ghosh** is originally from the United Kingdom but now lives in Christchurch. A graduate of the Hagley Writers' Institute, Nod has published extensively overseas and in New Zealand, including *Landfall*, *JAAM* and *Tākahē*.

**Jordan Hamel** is a Pōneke-based writer, poet and performer. He is the co-editor of *Stasis Journal* and co-editor of a forthcoming *Climate Change Poetry Anthology* from Auckland University Press. He has words in the *Poetry NZ Yearbook*, *Landfall*, *The Spinoff Newsroom*, *Tākahē*, *Sport*, and elsewhere.

**Jacqueline Hogler** is Toronto born, and 'serves the Muses'. Most oft found amidst the foliage around her home in Taranaki, she enjoys pearl-diving, snake-handling, and reading metaphysical texts. Caught practicing astrology without a license, she retreated to a Tibetan lamasery. Her Navajo name means 'One-Who-Bicycles-In-Sand', and her friends call her 'The Commodore'.

**Kristan Horne** was born in Christchurch and moved to Taranaki as a child. After living in Texas for a few years she returned to the province to train as a Nurse. She is a senior nurse in the Intensive Care Unit at Taranaki Base Hospital. This is her first ever published poem. She is a Wilco obsessive.

**Tim Jones** lives in Wellington. He was awarded the New Zealand Society of Authors Te Puni Kaituhi O Aotearoa Janet Frame Memorial Award for Literature in 2010. He has published one novel, one novella, two short story collections and five poetry collections, and co-edited two poetry anthologies. His latest book is a climate fiction novella, *Where We Land* (The Cuba Press, 2019).

**Katherine Joyce** is the literary pseudonym of an experienced writer who has links to Clarks Beach. This is her first published poem under this nom de lettres. She hopes to launch her first volume of poetry in Papakura in 2021.

**Tu'u Lafaeli'alii** is another first time Samoan writer in print, having also responded to an advertisement for Kaupeka: New Māori and Pasifika Writing (forthcoming, Te Perehi o Mātatuhi Taranaki, 2021). organised by Perehi o Mātātuhi Taranaki. Following his curiosity, he is experimenting with writing in Samoan and English language. Tu'u hails from Savai'i and is currently an undergraduate at the University of Auckland living at home with his family in Ahuruhuru.

**Trevor M Landers** was born in Hāwera, grew up near Kaūpokonui-a-Turi, and was educated at Sacred Heart Manaia, Hawera High School and Victoria University of Wellington, the University of Canterbury, and Auckland University of Technology. His recent publications include *Heart of Joyful Fortune* (2019), and *Whetū Mārama: Ekphrastic Poems from the New Zealand International Film Festival 2020* (2021) and his *Drawn from Life: Poems and Illustrations* is forthcoming.

**Vana Manasiades** is a second-generation Greek poet, translator and lecturer at AUT. As co-editor of the *Seraph Press Translation Series*, she has edited and translated from the Greek for Ναυάγια/Καταφύγια: Shipwrecks/Shelters (2016) and co-edited *Tātai Whetū: Seven Māori Women Poets in Translation* (March 2018). Vana was born in Wellington in 1973.

**Selena Tusitala Marsh**, ONZM is a poet and academic, and was the New Zealand Poet Laureate for 2017–2019. She is an Associate Professor of English at the University of Auckland. Through her mother, Sailigi Tusitala, Marsh is of Samoan and Tuvaluan ancestry and through her father James Crosbie, she is of English, Scottish and

French descent. Marsh grew up in Avondale, Auckland, New Zealand and resides on Waiheke Island.

**Rachel McAlpine** is a writer and web content strategist. She is the author of 30 books including poetry, plays, novels, and books about writing. Her first volume of poetry was published in 1975, and her tenth in 2005. Besides her professional work, McAlpine writes two personal blogs. She lives in Wellington, dances with the Crows Feet Dance Collective, walks a lot and does Tai Chi. She also lobbies for plain language communication from government agencies.

**Francien Mula** is currently a first year Biomedical Sciences student at the University of Auckland who loves creative writing on the side. As my daily life consists of science-heavy content, arts/literature, especially poetry is her favourite escape from my hectic life. It allows me to express her thoughts and feelings which can be effectively cathartic at times, she reports.

**Jeena Murphy** has worked as a print journalist, written TV comedy skits, wrote and produced Radio New Zealand Insight and Spectrum documentaries, published stories in *The New Zealand School Journal,* and short story anthologies. She's currently working on a novel trilogy set in 1930s France. The rest of her time's gobbled up by her teenage kids and running her business.

**Takunda Muzondiwa** is young Zimbabwean poet based in New Zealand. Her spoken word poetry continues to make waves nationally and globally. Through spoken

word, Takunda expresses the importance of identity as a tool for both self-empowerment and for the betterment of one's own community. She is currently a first year university student pursuing a Bachelor of Laws and Sociology in Auckland.

**Mikaela Nyman** is a Taranaki-based writer of fiction, non-fiction and poetry, with poems published in *Sport, Turbine, Minarets, Sweet Mammalian and Blackmail Press*. Her first novel, *Sado* (VUP) was published in 2020. Her first poetry collection När vändkrets läggs mot vändkrets (Ellips) was published in Finland in 2019. She is currently editing a Vanuatu women's anthology (forthcoming).

**Vira Paky** is a Congolese-Kiwi playwright, poet, and storyteller. Vira's work primarily focuses on herself, her relationships with others and the wider world. Her creative and vibrant perspective touches on the evolution of first-generation African migrant identity, her exploration of her black femininity and the plight of living inside and within broken systems.

**Lisette Prendé** is an actor, author and tarot reader from Wellington. She has contributed to publications such as *Headland Journal, The Spinoff and Stuff*. Lisette released her first novel, *Bianca De Lumiere*, in August 2020.

**Essa May Ranapiri** (Ngāti Wehi Wehi, Ngāti Raukawa, Waikato-Tainui, Te Arawa, Ngāti Pukeko, Na Guinnich, Highgate) is a poet from Kirikiriroa. Their first book of poetry, *Ransack* (VUP) was longlisted for the Ockham Awards 2020. They are the featured writer in *Poetry New Zealand Yearbook 2020* with their work 'HAUNT|HUNT'. Currently they are working on their second book of poems tentatively titled *Echidna*. They will write until dead.

**Richard Reeve** is an Otago-Dunedin poet. He has published six books of poetry, most recently, *Horse and Sheep* (Maungatua Press, 2019) and, *Generation Kitchen* (Otago University Press 2015). He lives in Warrington with Octavia and Koshka.

**Jack Ross** has published five poetry collections, three novels, three novellas, and three books of short fiction, most recently *Ghost Stories* (Lasavia Publishing, 2019). He was managing editor of *Poetry New Zealand* from 2014-2019, and has edited numerous other books, anthologies, and literary journals. He lives in Mairangi Bay on Auckland's North Shore, and teaches creative writing at Massey University.

**James Sagapolutele** is a 22 year old New Zealand Samoan courier driver from Papakura. James has recently discovered he enjoys writing in Samoan as a way of connecting with this heritage and culture. This is his first publication: 'A friend of mine at AUT flicked me the flyer Trevor send for Kaupeka: New Māori and Pasifika and I emailed him and here I am in this collection! Pretty cool, eh?'

**Sierra Southam** is a playwright, dreamer and all-aroundnerd who loves to tell stories that come from real experiences. When she's not writing, she can be found travelling in her van and playing with her dog.

**Ronnie Smart** is a poet and writer of short dark fiction. His writing has been published in numerous literary and genre
venues, including *Flash Frontier, Blue Fifth Review, Takahē, Breach, The Quick Brown Fox,* and the poetry anthology, *Untimely Frost*. He is currently waiting for an opportunity to travel to Niue to go scuba diving.

**Elvisa Van Der Leden** is a general creative, environmental educator and local government representative, Elvisa draws inspiration from the many hats she wears and spaces she traverses. Elvisa has been a natural creative since she was very young; writing poetry and music as a communication and therapy tool.

**Richard von Sturmer** was born on Auckland's North Shore in 1957. He is a writer, performer and filmmaker. His latest book, *Postcard Stories*, was published by Titus Books in 2019. He was the 2020 writer in residence at the University of Waikato. Currently he is working with filmmaker and musician Gabriel White as The Floral Clocks.

**Mercedes Webb-Pullman** started writing in 2007, and graduated from the International Institute of Modern Letters, Victoria University Wellington New Zealand with her MA in Creative Writing in 2011. Her work appears online and in print in NZ, Australia, Canada, USA, UK, Ireland, Spain, France, Germany, and

Palestine. Her published works are available for online purchase.

**Virginia Winder** wrote her first poem aged 12, the year she vowed to become a journalist. The most important poem she has written was called, 'I don't want you to be an if only.' It gained her a husband. She was twenty-five. The most powerful poem she has written was called 'This Too Shall Pass'. It won her the 2019 WOMAD Poetry Slam title. She was 56. She is still a journalist, and still married.

www.ingramcontent.com/pod-product-compliance
Lightning Source LLC
Chambersburg PA
CBHW051601010526
44118CB00023B/2782